Contar: De tres en tres
Counting by: Threes

Esther Sarfatti

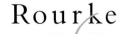

Rourke
Publishing LLC
Vero Beach, Florida 32964

www.rourkepublishing.com

PHOTO CREDITS: © Eileen Hart: title page and pages 5 and 21; © Jean Frooms: page 3; © James Steidl: page 7;
© Christine Balderas: page 9; © Ramona Heim: page 11; © Jason Lugo: page 13; © Michael Ledray: page 19;
© Terry Reimink: page 23.

Editor: Robert Stengard-Olliges

Cover design by Nicola Stratford.

Library of Congress Cataloging-in-Publication Data

Sarfatti, Esther.
  [Counting by threes. Spanish]
  Contar de tres en tres / Esther Sarfatti.
      p. cm. -- (Conceptos)
  ISBN 978-1-60044-749-5
  1. Counting--Juvenile literature. I. Title.
  QA113.S356318 2008
  513.2'11--dc22
                                        2007022531

Printed in the USA

CG/CG

Rourke Publishing

www.rourkepublishing.com – rourke@rourkepublishing.com
Post Office Box 3328, Vero Beach, FL 32964

Aquí hay tres.
This is three.

¿Cuantos grupos de tres puedes encontrar?

How many groups of threes can you find?

tres

3

3

Three

Three

tres

Un semáforo tiene tres luces.

A traffic light has three lights.

7

Un triciclo tiene tres ruedas.

A tricycle has three wheels.

Un triángulo tiene tres lados.

A triangle has three sides.

Esta bandera tiene
tres colores.

This flag has three colors.

Este pez payaso tiene
tres rayas.

This clownfish has three stripes.

Este helado tiene tres bolas.

This sundae has three scoops.

Este lagarto tiene
tres cuernos.

This lizard has three horns.

Esta familia tiene tres hijos.

This family has three kids.

Estos tres niños son trillizos.
¡Es divertido contar de tres
en tres!

These three kids are triplets.
Counting by threes is fun!

23

Índice

Index

Lecturas adicionales / Further Reading

Fitzkee, Jeremy. *One, Two, Three, Me.* Viking Penguin, 2006.
Jacobson, David. *Three Wishes.* Sterling, 2006.

Páginas Web recomendadas / Recommended Websites

www.edhelper.com/kindergarten/Number_3.htm
www.enchantedlearning.com/languagebooks/spanish/
numbers/

Acerca de la autora / About the Author

Esther Sarfatti lleva más de 15 años trabajando con libros infantiles como editora y traductora. Ésta es su primera serie como autora. Nacida en Brooklyn, Nueva York, donde creció en una familia trilingüe, Esther vive actualmente en Madrid, España, con su esposo y su hijo.

Esther Sarfatti has worked with children's books for over 15 years as an editor and translator. This is her first series as an author. Born in Brooklyn, New York, and brought up in a trilingual home, Esther currently lives with her husband and son in Madrid, Spain.

24